Haul in the Fish

By Sally Cowan

Contents

Eating Sea Food

People like to eat fish and other sea food.

We can eat raw fish.

Or we can fry up fish and chips!

But who goes out and
hauls in all that fish?

Nets and Traps

At dawn, big fishing boats
go out to sea.

The crew drop nets
into the sea.

Then, they haul up the nets.

The nets are filled with fish!

The crew pack the fish
into crates.

Then, they drop the nets in
again and haul up more fish.

On some boats, the crew
go fishing for prawns and crabs.

They haul in long nets
filled with prawns.

They put big traps down
in the sea to get crabs.

The crabs crawl into the traps.

This crab has big claws!

Look Out for Gulls!

Lots of hungry sea gulls fly to the nets.

They squawk and try to steal some fish!

Going Fishing

Kids can look for prawns with nets, too.

And kids can go fishing.

When the fishing line is loose, there is no fish.

But when the line is taut, there could be a fish on the end!

If you don't haul in any fish,
you can get fresh fish
in shops.

You can get prawns
and crabs, too.

Fish for All

Many other animals eat fish.
We must not haul in
too much fish from the sea!

Then there will be lots of fish
for all of us.

CHECKING FOR MEANING

1. What do the crew do with fish they catch in nets? *(Literal)*

2. Where can you get fresh fish from? *(Literal)*

3. Why do you think fishing boats go out at dawn? *(Inferential)*

EXTENDING VOCABULARY

dawn	What time of day is *dawn*? What other words do you know for times in the day? E.g. dusk, evening, morning, afternoon.
prawns	What does a *prawn* look like? How might you describe a prawn? Where do they live?
taut	What is meant by *But when the line is taut, there could be a fish on the end!*? What does *taut* mean? What is the opposite of *taut*?

MOVING BEYOND THE TEXT

1. What other food do we get from the sea? Do you like sea food?

2. Do you think you would like to work on a fishing boat? Why or why not?

3. Where else might you find sea gulls?

4. What do you think is important to do to stay safe if you go fishing?

DIPHTHONGS

| oy | ow | oo | aw |

PRACTICE WORDS

raw

hauls

dawn

prawns

haul

crawl

taut

claws